SPEAKING of BLENDS...

A Book by a Speech Language Pathologist

Fulton Books
Meadville, PA

Published by Fulton Books 2023

ISBN 979-8-88505-771-4 (paperback)
ISBN 979-8-88505-772-1 (digital)

Printed in the United States of America

DEDICATION

This book is dedicated to two of my mentors who are pioneers in their fields: **Dr. Reem Khamis and Dr. Gilbert Foley.**

Dr. Reem Khamis is a researcher, professor, and activist within the communication sciences and disorders field. She was one of the few in the field who saw my potential and guided me along the way as we collaborated on studies that focused on bilingual children and empowering families from minority groups in the US.

Dr. Gilbert Foley is a brilliant mind who finds joy and passion in sharing his knowledge with others. His modesty, passion, and resilience within the field reflect the best qualities of a leader and a mentor.

Thank you both for believing in me. I hope that this book will make you proud.

Let's see if you can spy the hidden objects in the classroom!

Good morning, friends! Today we are going to learn about—
Miss Iman! I pie a pider!
I'm so fared!

Oh! I see the spider now.
Let's fray it!
Oh, no need to spray the spider, Abby!
Let's open up the window so that it can escape.
Bye, pider!
PAM

3

All right, class, today we are going to learn about S blends! S blends occur when the sssss sound gets paired together with another consonant sound like P!
Ssssp! Sssspider.
4

It's important that we say both sounds in the blend because otherwise, we'd be changing the word. For instance:
Pot
Spot
Pin
Spin

I'm going to pass around some mirrors so that we can practice together.

First, smile with your teeth and make a long stretchy sssss sound.

Next, put your lips together and feel the air build up behind your lips.

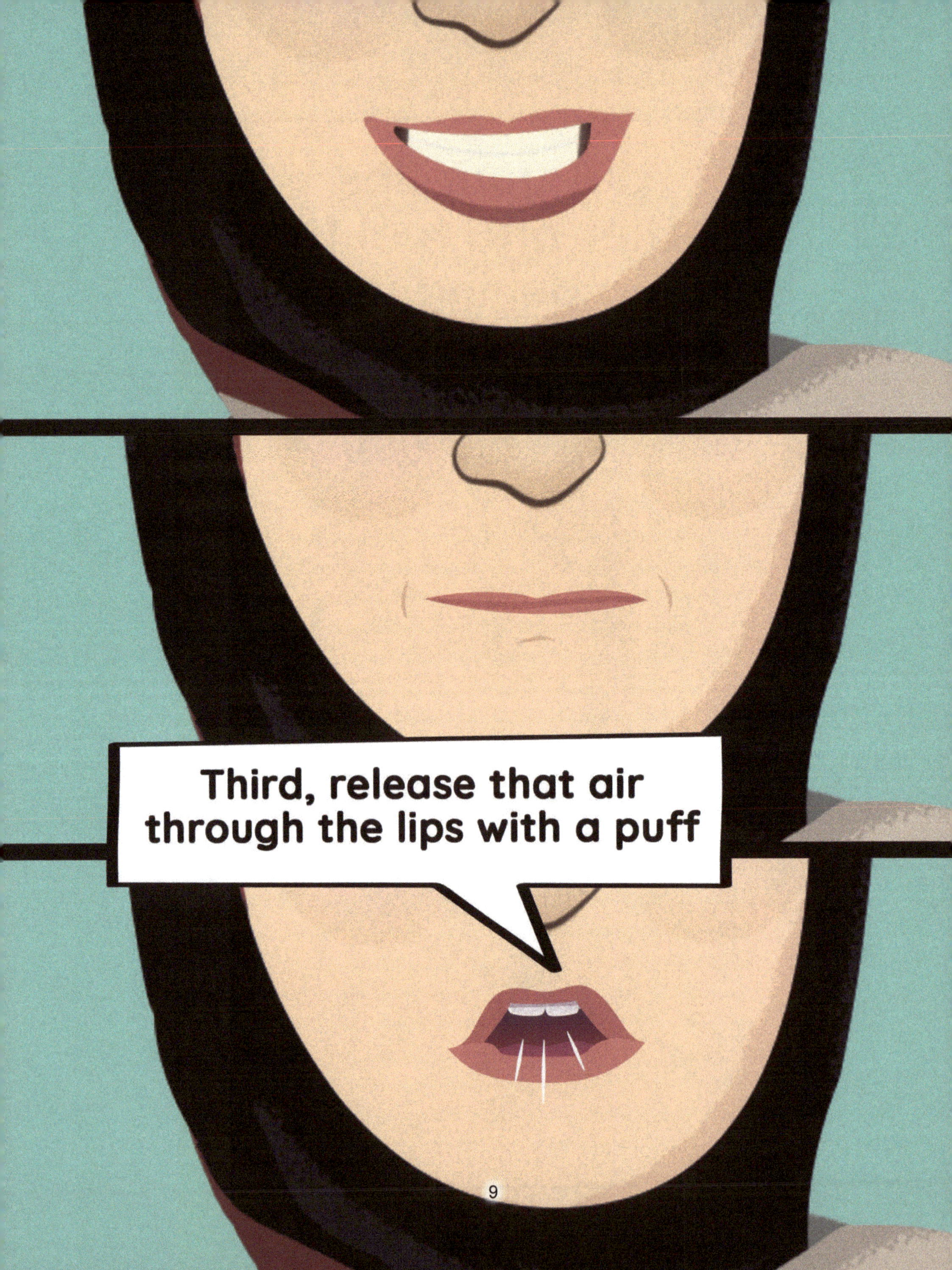
Third, release that air
through the lips with a puff

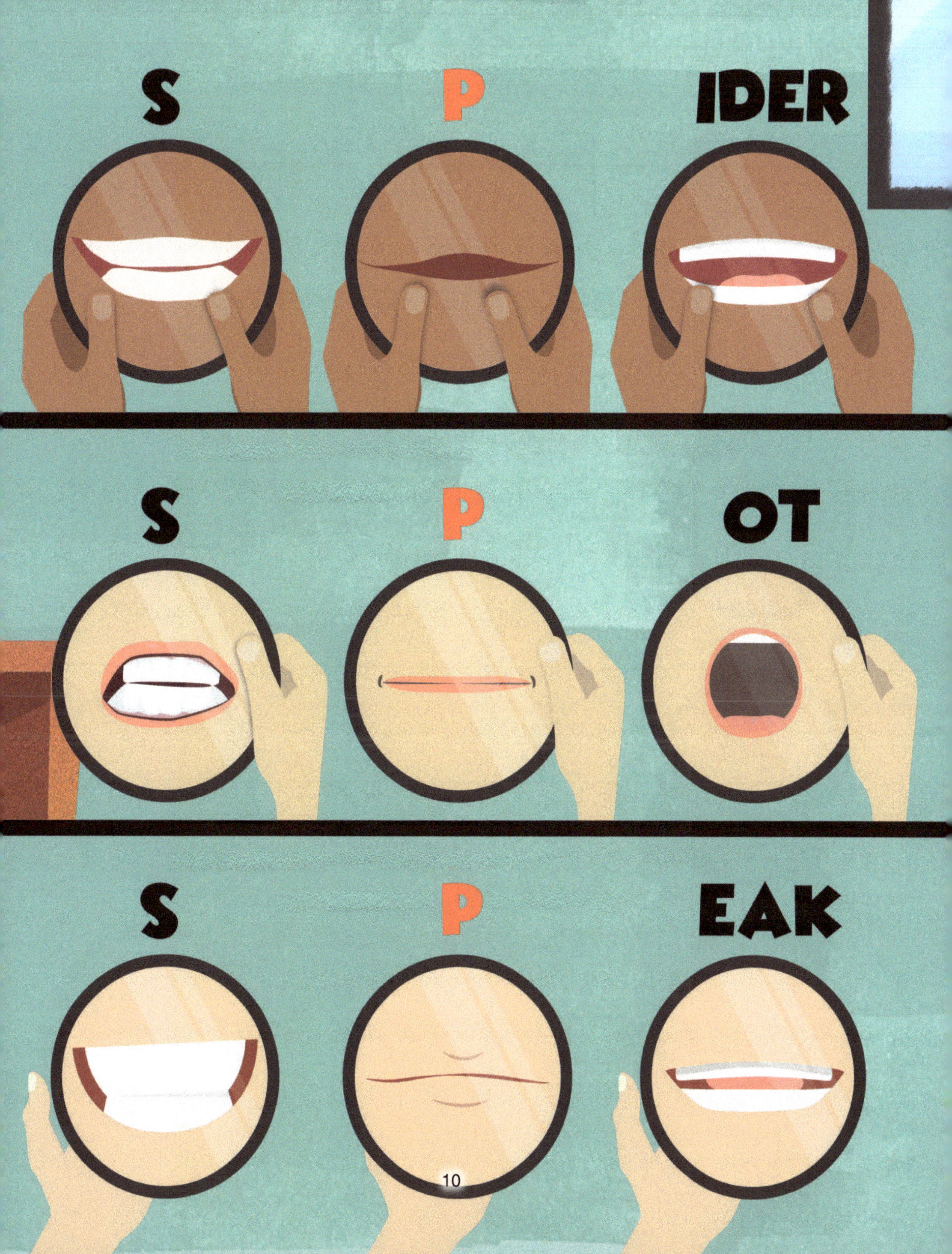
S P IDER
S P OT
S P EAK
10

As you make the /s/ sound,
drag your finger along the dots
until the end! Then tap the P as
you make the /p/ sound.

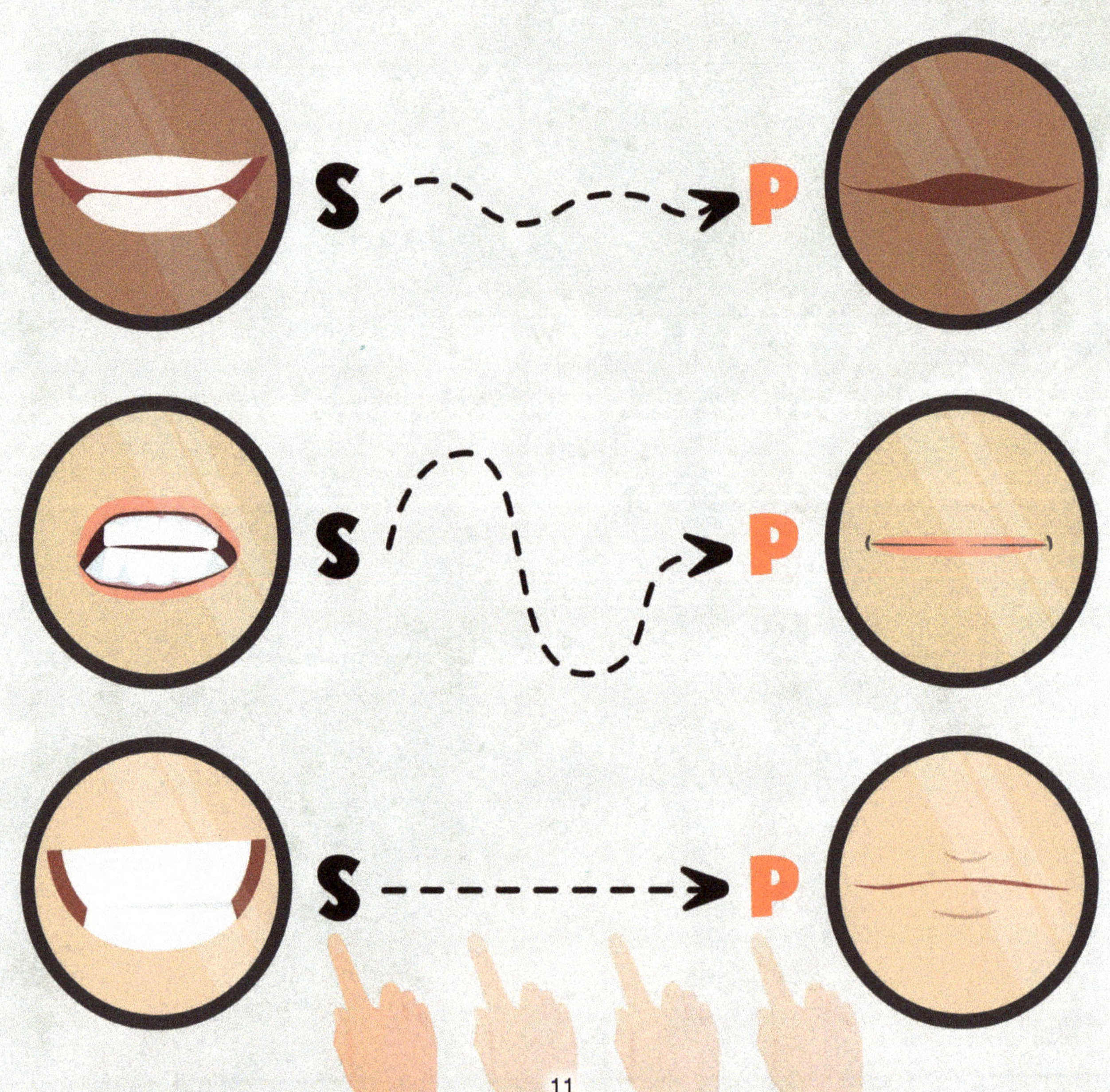

We did it!
SPLENDID!

Hey Miss Iman, is it lunch time yet?
I want some Sittles
I think Miss Perez can help with that.
I want to eat Sake
And I want some pies
Sickers!
Spaghetti!

Were you able to find all the hidden objects in the classroom?
SPAM

Meet the Author

Iman Salam

Iman Salam is an Arab American who pursued speech and language pathology as well as infant mental health and developmental practices.

Iman grew up in Lebanon before moving to the States at the age of thirteen. Having to adapt to novel and challenging environments while at the same time preserving her identity, Iman became passionate about empowering children from minority backgrounds as well as children with disabilities and those who have experienced war trauma.

Meet the Illustartor

Fatima Salam

Fatima Salam is a Lebanese Filipino graphic designer and illustrator who is passionate about story-telling through her visuals.

www.ingramcontent.com/pod-product-compliance
Lightning Source LLC
Chambersburg PA
CBHW041828110726
48006CB00019B/2550